IMAGES
of America

COLD WAR
ALABAMA

ON THE COVER: Born in 1935 in Alexander City, Lt. William "Bill" H. Wood Jr. kneels in front of his T-33 trainer aircraft. After graduating from Mellow Valley High School, he went to the Alabama Polytechnic Institute in Auburn. Following college, he commissioned in the US Air Force and became a pilot. He went through instructor training at Craig Air Force Base in Selma, Alabama. In 1966, he deployed for a tour in Vietnam as an airborne forward air controller. Upon return, Wood served, as an Air Force officer, in National Aeronautics and Space Administration's manned Spacecraft Center in Houston, Texas, where he developed lunar surface procedures for the Apollo 11 mission. (Courtesy of Alabama Department of Archives and History.)

IMAGES
of America

COLD WAR
ALABAMA

Melvin G. Deaile, PhD

ARCADIA
PUBLISHING

Copyright © 2024 by Melvin G. Deaile, PhD
ISBN 978-1-4671-6079-7

Published by Arcadia Publishing
Charleston, South Carolina

Printed in the United States of America

Library of Congress Control Number: 2023940712

For all general information, please contact Arcadia Publishing:
Telephone 843-853-2070
Fax 843-853-0044
E-mail sales@arcadiapublishing.com

Visit us on the Internet at www.arcadiapublishing.com

To those in Alabama and across the United States who endeavored,
fought, and persevered to build a "more perfect Union"

CONTENTS

Acknowledgments

I would like to thank Arcadia Publishing, specifically Lindsey Givens, for reaching out and gauging my interest in completing this project. Special thanks go to Amy Jarvis, my editor from Arcadia Publishing, who kept me on track and offered valued insight. I would also like to thank Amelia Chase, Alabama Department of Archives and History, for her support and help in finding images critical to the completion of this book. Lastly, a special thanks goes to editor Lisa Yambrick for making all my works better.

To my kids, Faith Terket, Melvin Deaile, and Joy Deaile, thank you for your continued support of my endeavor to preserve history for later generations. For my son-in-law, Nick Terket, I appreciate your service to the nation and in the new "Cold War" against Russia.

Finally, I am thankful for the love, support, and encouragement of my biggest fan: my wife, Manda.

The conclusions and opinions expressed in this manuscript are those of the author and do not necessarily reflect the official policy or position of the US government, Department of Defense, or the Air University.

INTRODUCTION

The Cold War began almost immediately after the end of World War II. Despite having been allies during World War II, the Soviet Union and the United States would enter a new conflict that would last almost for almost 50 years. George Kennan, a diplomat serving in Russia after the war, was the first to sound the alarm about what he perceived to be the expansionist desires of the Soviet Union. Unlike the previous war, this war became a contest between ideologies. It was a struggle to determine the best form of government—capitalism and democracy, or communism and a government command economy. The conflict earned the moniker "Cold War" because it never turned "hot," meaning that there was never direct conflict between the two countries. This does not mean that there wasn't contestation and competition throughout the five decades. While military might played a significant role in the conflict, it expanded to several other fronts.

As World War II drew to a close, the United States demonstrated its ability to weaponize the power of the atom. The bombings of the Japanese cities of Hiroshima and Nagasaki with newly developed atomic weapons brought an end to World War II and ushered in the nuclear age. During the initial years of the Cold War, the United States enjoyed a monopoly on nuclear weapons. For a short time, the US Air Force's strategic bombers and nuclear weapons served as a deterrent to the Soviet Union's overwhelming conventional capability. In 1949, the Soviet Union demonstrated its ability to develop a nuclear weapon, changing the character of the war. Through almost the first decade of the Cold War, the bombers and bombs stood as the main deterrent for both nations. In 1957, an event occurred that would shift the nature of the war once again.

On October 4, 1957, Russia would launch the first artificial satellite, Sputnik, into space, with great strategic implications. Under President Eisenhower's administration, the development of ballistic missiles took center stage. "Ike" feared that Russia could eventually put a nuclear weapon on top of a missile and deliver it in a matter of minutes (which both nations would do). The United States lagged Russia in missile development, and Ike asked the services to solve the problem. The Army's Redstone Arsenal in Huntsville, Alabama, would play a role in Eisenhower's drive for a ballistic missile that could deliver a nuclear weapon.

Russia had an encore for its historic first: On April 12, 1961, the Russians would launch the first human, Yuri Gagarin, into space. America was behind not only in the missile development, but in the space race as well. In a 1961 address before Congress, Pres. John F. Kennedy would establish a new national space objective. At Rice University in Houston, Texas, in 1962, the president established a goal of reaching the Moon within a decade. This strategic focus had implications for Alabama, as the Marshall Space Flight Center in Huntsville became the center for producing the propulsion necessary to reach the Moon.

While the United States struggled politically to prove democracy a better political system than communism, it had problems at home. Jim Crow laws, segregation, and voting abuses within America prevented the country from realizing the ideal of a "more perfect union." The situation also served as propaganda for the Soviet Union, which sought to exploit the inequalities within the so-called beacon of democracy as a way to sway sympathizers in the United States, and globally, to their side.

Even though the Soviet Union and the United States never had a direct conflict during the Cold War, that does not mean wars were not fought. While the US military continued to prepare for the possibility of all-out nuclear war with the Soviet Union, it fought small wars overseas to contain the spread of communism. In places like Korea and Vietnam, US forces fought to prevent democratic governments from falling to communism. After major fighting in the Korean War (1950–1953) ended with a cease fire (technically, the war continues to this day), the Army developed a new tactic for these small wars using helicopters to bring troops to the battle. The emphasis on helicopters in the Army would have huge implications for Alabama's Fort Rucker, the Army's aviation center.

Everything in the Cold War was a competition. Much like the in-state football rivalry between Alabama and Auburn, the competitive nature of the Cold War extended beyond the military and political arenas. The Olympics became a way to showcase which country had the better system. Competition between the two rivals occurred from the swimming pool to track and field events. It was also a contest between culture and lifestyles. From commerce to television programs, America tried to highlight the benefits of the "nuclear family" and domestically made products, which Alabama had a hand in producing. Not everyone, however, supported US policies. Groups of college students in Alabama joined their counterparts across the country to protest the Vietnam War and demand change. The Cold War permeated every facet of American life, and Alabama was no exception.

In 1989, the Berlin Wall, separating West Berlin from East Berlin, would fall, signaling the beginning of the end of the Cold War. While the "wall" began to fall under Ronald Reagan's presidency, it would take several years for both sides to acknowledge the end of global competition. By 1991, with George H.W. Bush the president, the Cold War would end with the United States emerging victorious. This book recounts, through images, Alabama's contribution to that victory.

One

THE DETERRENCE FRONT
BOMBERS TO MISSILES

In the aftermath of World War II, Germany was essentially split into two sides—East and West—with the Soviet Union having primary control over East Germany. The capital city, which was situated in East Germany, also was split into East and West Berlin. In 1948, Soviet Premier Joseph Stalin closed off Western access to West Berlin. Having been cut off from overland access, the survival of West Berlin became reliant on a Western airlift operation that kept the city's residents fed. The effort lasted almost an entire year before Stalin lifted the restrictions. The Berlin Airlift became the first "battle" in the Cold War. Knowing the Soviet Union's intentions to try and spread its influence across Europe, the United States had to develop a way to deter it. Deterrence is essentially threatening an adversary with coercive force to prevent them from taking an action.

The United States ended World War II as the sole nuclear power in the world. Rather than conscripting a large army, the Americans decided to rely on strategic bombers and nuclear weapons as the primary way to deter Soviet aggression. Strategic Air Command became the military organization charged with executing the "atomic air offensive" if Russia tried to make a move on Western Europe. In 1949, the Soviet Union detonated its own nuclear device. This development changed the character of the Cold War; many feared what would happen if nuclear weapons could be mounted on ballistic missiles and used to attack targets in a matter of minutes. President Eisenhower made ballistic missile development, in which the United States trailed the Soviet Union, a national priority. Redstone Arsenal in Huntsville, Alabama, worked toward fulfilling the president's national security objective.

The first atomic weapon employed by the United States was the "Little Boy" bomb. This uranium-based weapon, whose design was never tested before its use, was dropped on August 6, 1945. The B-29 Superfortress bomber, nicknamed *Enola Gay*, delivered its nuclear payload on the Japanese town of Hiroshima shortly after 8:00 a.m. local time. (Courtesy of the US Air Force.)

A Boeing B-29 Superfortress, like the one pictured above, delivered the only atomic weapons used in war. Brought into service toward the end of World War II, the B-29s were the first pressurized bombers, which allowed them to reach higher bombing altitudes. B-29s would also see service in the Korean War, as they were the only operational bomber that Gen. Curtis LeMay, the Strategic Air Command commander, would allow to deploy to the Far East. (Courtesy of the US Air Force.)

During the initial decade of the Cold War, bombers were the only platform capable of delivering a nuclear weapon; therefore, they were the initial deterrent force. The Convair B-36 Peacemaker became the backbone of the nuclear bomber fleet because of its ability to take off from the United States, fly unrefueled to its target in the Soviet Union, deliver its payload, and return to the United States. One reason for this capability is that the B-36 was initially designed to travel the long bombing distances required during World War II; however, the plane never served in action. Initially designed with six propellers, four jet engines were later added to give it increased speed. The bomber earned the nickname "Six turning and four burning" for its engine configuration. (Courtesy of the US Air Force.)

The Boeing B-47 Stratojet eventually replaced the B-36 as the main bomber in the US deterrent force. The B-47's six jet engines modeled the Air Force's plan to transition to an all-jet bomber force. The bomber had a three-person crew: a bombardier in the nose, a pilot in the middle, and a copilot in the aft seat. The seating arrangement gave the plane its nickname "the three-headed stepchild." (Courtesy of the US Air Force.)

Since the B-47 bomber lacked the range of its predecessor, the B-36, the Air Force had to develop an in-flight refueling capability. Although variants of the B-29 served as the initial in-flight refueling platform, the Boeing KC-97 Stratofreighter was the first dedicated refueler. The boom in the aft of the plane would extend in air and deliver gas to the waiting bomber. (Courtesy of the US Air Force.)

Pictured above are the two aircraft that were the mainstay of the bomber deterrent fleet in Strategic Air Command. The eight-engine Boeing B-52 Stratofortress came into service during the 1950s and continues service to this day. Until the 1990s, the B-52 had a crew of six: a radar navigator (bombardier) and navigator on the initial deck, and a pilot, copilot, electronic warfare officer, and gunner on the top deck. Following Operation Desert Storm and the end of the Cold War, the Air Force eliminated the gunner position. The Boeing KC-135 Stratotanker, seen refueling the B-52, was a four-jet-engine refueler that provided bombers the gas needed to reach their targets in the Soviet Union. Initially, the KC-135 had a crew of four—pilot, copilot, navigator, and boom operator. The development of the global positioning system eventually resulted in the elimination of the navigator position. (Courtesy of the US Air Force.)

Pictured above is a replica of the Semyorka rocket (R-7) that launched the Sputnik satellite into orbit on October 4, 1957. The event not only ignited the space race but also started the ballistic missile race. Both sides of the Cold War saw the potential to put nuclear weapons on ballistic weapons and deliver the payloads on their adversary's target in a matter of minutes. (Courtesy of Sergei Korolyov in VDNH, Ostankino, Moscow.)

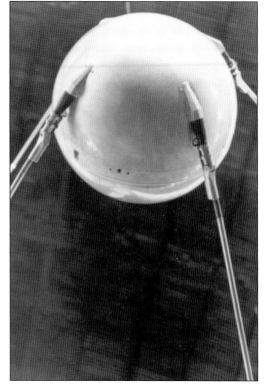

The first country to explore space was Russia. The Semyorka rocket enabled its payload, the satellite named Sputnik (pictured above), to enter low Earth orbit, where it remained for roughly three weeks. During that time, it sent radio signals down to Earth. Eventually, drag overcame Sputnik's orbit, and it fell back to Earth. (Courtesy of NASA.)

Headquarters, Redstone Arsenal,
Huntsville, Alabama

President Eisenhower made ballistic missile acquisition his top priority because of Sputnik. One place that would help develop that capability was Redstone Arsenal, which was initially established in the leadup to World War II as a chemical weapons manufacturing and storage facility. It was located close to Huntsville, Alabama. (Courtesy of the US Army.)

Following World War II, ammunition production at Redstone stopped. In 1950, the secretary of the Army, Frank Pace, decided to transfer its rocket research division to the arsenal in Huntsville. Members of the division, including Dr. Wernher von Braun, were part of Operation Paperclip, a secret intelligence program that brought highly intelligent German scientists to the United States. This photograph shows 104 of the scientists at Fort Bliss, Texas. When the group arrived at Huntsville, missile development began. (Courtesy of the US Army.)

The Hermes test rocket, shown above, was a liquid-fueled rocket that was used primarily for research purposes. Project Hermes was among the first US attempts to develop a rocket program. When the Germans began launching V-2 rockets in World War II, the United States had to evaluate its rocket force needs. Armed with the knowledge of this program, the members of Project Paperclip would begin work on rockets in Huntsville, Alabama. (Courtesy of the US Army.)

The rocket division immediately began working on several programs. One of those programs, Lacrosse, was a Marine short-range rocket system. The Defense Department decided that short-range systems should be assigned to Army at Redstone. Lacrosse was a short-range surface-to-surface system extending the artillery capability in support of ground forces. (Courtesy of the US Army.)

James Van Allen of the University of Iowa holds a Loki missile. Loki was another Redstone project, but instead of supporting troops, this was an anti-aircraft missile. The initial tests of Loki demonstrated the advantages of solid rocket-propelled systems. Unlike liquid-fueled systems, solid rocket motors cannot vary thrust output or restart. Once a solid rocket motor is ignited, it burns until exhaustion. The advantage of solid rocket systems is the ease of storage. After significant testing, the Army eventually abandoned the program in favor of other projects. The Navy, however, put a chaff payload in the Loki rockets, firing them to high altitude. When the chaff dispersed, the Navy could track the metallic objects and calibrate radars or gain information on high-altitude wind speeds. (Courtesy of NASA.)

Assigned to the Army at Redstone in the 1950s, the Hawk surface-to-air missile targeted low-altitude penetrating aircraft. Besides its low- to medium-altitude capability, the Hawk missile system demonstrated the ability to maneuver on the modern battlefield. The Army would field the Hawk system, and the Marines would deploy it shortly afterward. Foreign countries would receive versions of Hawk as well. US forces never fired the Hawk in combat, but the Israelis used the system to shoot down attacking aircraft in the 1967 Six-Day War. Furthermore, Kuwaitis used an improved variant of the Hawk system (I-Hawk) to target Iraqi aircraft during the leadup to Operation Desert Storm. (Courtesy of the US Army.)

While Redstone worked on a number of short-to-intermediate-range missile systems, President Eisenhower wanted an intercontinental ballistic missile capability, which became the mission of the US Air Force. The newly formed Army Ballistic Missile Agency (ABMA) in Huntsville designed the first rocket, named Redstone, to carry a live nuclear warhead. The Redstone missile never achieved intercontinental distances and was deployed as a deterrent in Western Europe. The discoveries from Redstone would fuel the follow-on program. (Courtesy of the US Army.)

The Redstone missile, named for the Redstone Arsenal, about to be test-flown over the Air Force Test Center Range. The gantry tower beside the missile is used in preflight preparations. Redstone saw service in Germany from June 1958 until June 1964. Technology and lessons from the Redstone program fueled other derivatives. The Mercury-Redstone rocket would carry the first US astronaut, Alan Shepard, into space. (Courtesy of Alabama Department of Archives and History.)

The Jupiter program was a follow-on to the Redstone rocket program. The Jupiter missile could deliver a nuclear warhead more than 1,000 nautical miles (considered a medium-range ballistic missile). Jupiter would eventually be deployed to US allies in Western Europe (Italy and Turkey) since it could not reach its targets from US soil. The deployment of Jupiter missiles became a part of the negotiations during the Cuban Missile Crisis. (Courtesy of NASA.)

Redstone Arsenal received a lot of statewide and nationwide attention. Here, the future governor of Alabama, John Patterson, shakes hands with Karl Hanchey, a welder at Redstone Arsenal, in August 1958. At the time, Patterson was the attorney general until his election as governor in the fall of 1958. (Courtesy of Alabama Department of Archives and History.)

Redstone Arsenal had the nation's largest static test firing stand for rocket motors. When constructed, the facility cost nearly $12 million. Built with reinforced concrete, the structure stands over 15 stories high. In order to test the missile's engine, the missile is locked in place and the rocket motor fired. (Courtesy of Alabama Department of Archives and History.)

Col. John C. Nickerson, a World War II veteran, met Dr. Von Braun while working in Washington, DC. He moved to Redstone Arsenal to work on the Jupiter rocket program for the Army Ballistic Missile Agency. In 1956, Secretary of Defense Charles Wilson decided that the Army would focus on short-range ballistic missiles while the USAF concentrated on Intercontinental Ballistic Missiles (ICBMs). Upset over the decision, Nickerson leaked his concerns in print to the press and would eventually be charged with violations of the Espionage Act (the final verdict was suspension of rank for a year). (Courtesy of Alabama Department of Archives and History. Donated by Alabama Media Group. Photograph by Norman Dean, Birmingham News.)

As the Cold War heated up, Secretary of Defense Charles Wilson assigned each of the services certain roles to avoid duplication of effort. The Air Force would focus on long-range ballistic missiles as well as long-range bombers. While initially part of the Jupiter program, the Navy went its own way to pursue the Polaris missile, which was capable of delivering a nuclear payload. The Army's missile program, under the Army Ballistic Missile Agency, stayed focused on homeland defense. The Nike-Hercules surface-to-air missile typically had a nuclear warhead (W-31) and was deployed to defend strategic sites in the United States. This Nike-Hercules missile was displayed at the Alabama State Fair in Birmingham in 1958. (Courtesy of Alabama Department of Archives and History. Donated by Alabama Media Group. Photograph by Tom Self, Birmingham News.)

A Zeus missile, which was part of the Nike family of missiles, sits in front of the Goddard house, an old plantation home that the Army took possession of when it established the arsenal in Huntsville in the 1940s. (Courtesy of Alabama Department of Archives and History.)

Missiles for Defense

As the Air Force focused on ballistic missiles, the Army produced short- and mid-range ballistic missiles as well as nuclear-capable missiles to defend the homeland. Pictured here is the family of missiles developed by Redstone and the Army Ballistic Missile Agency for that mission. (Courtesy of Alabama Department of Archives and History.)

The Pershing missile was another follow-on to the Redstone missile. The missile was named after famed Gen. John "Black Jack" Pershing, who led the American Expeditionary Forces during World War I. It would be capable of delivering a nuclear weapon deep into enemy territory. (Courtesy of the US Army.)

The Pershing surface-to-surface missile, another Redstone program, could deliver a nuclear warhead into enemy territory. When placed in Western Europe, the missile could reach Moscow. This drew the concerns of the Soviet leadership. In 1986, Pres. Ronald Reagan and Soviet general secretary Mikhail Gorbachev negotiated the Intermediate-Range Nuclear Forces Treaty, which eliminated nuclear missiles with a range of 500 to 5,000 kilometers. (Courtesy of Alabama Department of Archives and History.)

The Pershing Missile, Redstone Arsenal

The advent of the missile age brought new threats beyond just military ones. The idea that American citizens could be attacked within a matter of minutes led the US government to produce several public service announcements to prepare its citizens for the possibility of attack. Pictured here is the cover of a survival manual. (Courtesy of the US government.)

Americans could use bomb shelters as a way to protect against nuclear attack. Pictured here are some abandoned bomb shelters on the Green Spring Highway in Birmingham, Alabama. The sign in the background reads, "Don't Die through H Bomb Blast, Radioactive Fallout, Tornadoes, Live! Radiation Shelters Inc." (Courtesy of Alabama Department of Archives and History. Donated by Alabama Media Group. Photograph by Anthony Falletta, Birmingham News.)

Another group of abandoned fallout shelters is seen along the Green Spring Highway in Birmingham. The signs on these structure read, "Another Bomb Shelter Built by C.E. Sawyer's Industrial Sheet Metal Fabrications." (Courtesy of Alabama Department of Archives and History. Donated by Alabama Media Group. Photograph by Anthony Falletta, Birmingham News.)

An individual identified as Harry McDonald stands with a set of abandoned fallout shelters at the Birmingham Tank Company on Twenty-seventh Avenue and Twenty-fifth North Street in Birmingham. The company was a division of Ingalls Iron Works. (Courtesy of Alabama Department of Archives and History. Donated by Alabama Media Group. Photograph by Anthony Falletta, Birmingham News.)

Two

THE SPACE FRONT
RACE TO THE MOON

The Soviet Union's launch of Sputnik on October 4, 1957, changed the character of the Cold War. Although both the Americans and the Soviets had nuclear weapons and bombers, the ballistic missile age had begun. The Army's Redstone Arsenal played a significant role in developing missiles for defending the homeland as well as delivering nuclear weapons into the enemy's territory.

Sputnik presented another challenge: the Soviet Union demonstrated it had surpassed the United States in the exploration of space. The Russians put the first artificial satellite into orbit and followed that feat with another first. On April 12, 1961, Russian cosmonaut Yuri Gagarin became the first human to orbit the Earth.

For the Eisenhower administration, ballistic missiles were a military mission, but President Eisenhower wanted a civilian agency to focus on space exploration. The National Aeronautics and Space Administration (NASA) assumed responsibility from the Army for space exploration activities in 1960.

In Huntsville, a separate civilian agency, the Marshall Space Flight Center, coexisted on Redstone Arsenal to work on the mission of exceeding Russian space capabilities. The German scientists who came to Redstone to work on ballistic missiles would also work for the Space Flight Center to help Pres. John F. Kennedy reach his goal of putting a man on the Moon within a decade. The engineers at Huntsville would play a big part in making that goal achievable. Rocket propulsion would be engineered and tested at Huntsville and then shipped to Florida for the actual launches.

The civilian agency at Huntsville responsible for the development of rockets for the space program was named for George C. Marshall. Marshall led a life of service to his nation. A stellar career in the Army ultimately led to him serving as the Army's chief of staff during World War II and earning a fifth star. Pres. Harry S. Truman asked him to serve as his secretary of state, which he did from 1947 to 1949. His efforts to develop the Marshall Plan as a financial and engagement plan to help Western Europe rebuild after the devastation of the war earned him a Nobel Peace Prize. He also was Truman's secretary of defense from 1950 to 1951. It was unprecedented for one person to hold these multiple roles in one lifetime. In this picture, Marshall's widow, Katherine, helps Pres. Dwight Eisenhower unveil Marshall's bust at the Space Center's dedication ceremony on September 8, 1960. (Courtesy of NASA.)

The first director of the Marshall Space Flight Center was Dr. Wernher von Braun. Raised in Nazi Germany, von Braun worked on rocket technology and the development of the V-2 rocket for the Third Reich. Following the war, von Braun secretly immigrated to the United States under Operation Paperclip, a classified intelligence program that helped nearly 1,600 German scientists and technology experts move to the United States to work on space programs. Von Braun was with the group of scientists that moved from Fort Bliss to Huntsville when the Army stood up the rocket division at Redstone. In 1960, he took over the civilian agency responsible for rocket production for NASA. For his efforts on the space program, Pres. Gerald R. Ford would award him the nation's highest scientific honor, the National Medal of Science in Engineering. (Courtesy of NASA.)

Hermann Oberth, the father of German rocketry, moved to Switzerland to continue his work on rockets following the war. He would join his protégé Wernher von Braun at Huntsville in 1955 to help the United States win the space race. (Courtesy of NASA.)

While rocket development occurred in Huntsville, some of the testing occurred elsewhere in the South. The Mississippi Test Facility, now called the Stennis Space Center, contributed to the success of the Apollo program. Due to noise concerns at the Huntsville test site, testing of the larger Apollo rocket motors moved to the Mississippi Test Facility. (Courtesy of NASA.)

Rockets developed at Huntsville had to get to Cape Canaveral, Florida, where rocket launches occurred. The *Palaemon* barge was responsible for transporting the rockets by waterways because they were too large to take by land. The barge was named for the Greek sea-god and the protector of ships. On April 17, 1961, the watercraft made its maiden voyage. The journey would take the rocket along the Tennessee River to the Ohio River and eventually down the Mississippi River. Exiting into the Gulf of Mexico, the barge would travel around the tip of Florida and up the Atlantic coast to Cape Canaveral. (Courtesy of Alabama Department of Archives and History.)

With each progressive space program (Mercury, Gemini, and Apollo), the number of people in the capsule grew from one (Mercury) to three (Apollo). Apollo, the program to put a man on the Moon, used the Saturn family of rockets. The Saturn I (pictured) was the first iteration of the rocket for the lunar mission. The Saturn V would take the astronauts to the Moon. (Courtesy of Alabama Department of Archives and History.)

The Saturn I liquid-fueled rocket pictured here was powered by six RL 10 engines using liquid oxygen and liquid hydrogen. The actual Saturn V rocket used on the Apollo 11 mission to the Moon had five F1 engines. (Courtesy of Alabama Department of Archives and History.)

Atlas Agena-B Space Vehicle with Ranger Spacecraft

Before putting a man on the Moon, NASA wanted images of the surface. The Atlas rocket pictured here was used to launch the Ranger spacecraft that would take the first up-close images of the Moon. Due to the reduced payload, the Atlas's two and half stages were sufficient to complete the mission of launching the Ranger. Launching the Rangers was the easy part of the mission. It took seven tries before the Ranger would send back images of the Moon. Some of the first six Rangers made it to the Moon only to miss their landing by a few kilometers. When Ranger 7 landed on the Moon, it technically "crashed" on the Moon (on purpose), but before its demise Ranger 7 sent back images better than any NASA had previously captured with telescopes. (Courtesy of Alabama Department of Archives and History.)

Before humans entered space, animals took the ride because of their similarities in physiology. Even before reaching the Moon, some looked beyond it to other adventures. Mars seemed like the next logical leap. In this picture, David Wilson (right), a college student working during the summer for Marshall Space Flight Laboratories, shows an unidentified space center employee a survival capsule designed to hold a monkey for the anticipated six-month journey to Mars. David loaned the capsule to the Marshall Space Flight Center for display since his design had won international acclaim. (Courtesy of Alabama Department of Archives and History.)

Getting into space was only part of the mission to the Moon. A way had to be devised for humans to breathe in space and on the Moon, which obviously did not have the atmosphere of Earth. In addition, a visor system had to be devised to protect human eyes from the direct sunlight they could be exposed to while in space or on the Moon. This picture was taken in Huntsville, Alabama. (Courtesy of Alabama Department of Archives and History.)

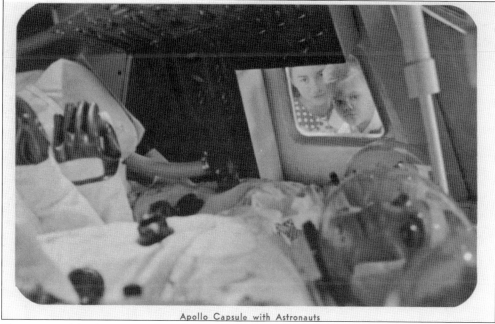

Apollo Capsule with Astronauts

These are models of astronauts from the Gemini program, the second of NASA's three space programs (Mercury, Gemini, and Apollo). In the Gemini program, the capsule carried two astronauts, who laid on their backs for takeoff. This position allowed the astronauts to better sustain the gravitational forces involved at launch than they could sitting upright. (Courtesy of Alabama Department of Archives and History.)

The United States initially lagged the Soviet Union in space exploration. Using the Jupiter ballistic missile, the United States finally launched its satellite, Explorer I, into space on February 1, 1958. Here, a group of space flight center personnel receive a briefing on Explorer I. Seated at the table are Dr. Eberhard Rees (an Operation Paperclip scientist who would take over the center after Wernher von Braun's retirement), Maj. Gen. Edmond O'Connor (US Army), and Dr. von Braun. Although the US satellite came after the Russian Sputnik, it was the spacecraft to detect the Van Allen radiation belt (a zone of charged particles captured in the Earth's magnetosphere). After four months, the batteries aboard Explorer I died, but the satellite remained in orbit until 1970. (Courtesy of NASA.)

The Ranger spacecraft sitting atop this Atlas rocket would provide the images of the Moon that NASA needed prior to a landing. While circling the Moon, the Ranger sent back over 4,000 photographs. The Marshall Space Flight Center provided the rockets for these missions to the Moon. (Courtesy of Alabama Department of Archives and History.)

President Kennedy set the nation on a course to the Moon in 1962. The following year, Kennedy visited Huntsville and the personnel at Redstone Arsenal as well as the Marshall Space Flight Center. He addressed the crowd on Armed Forces Day, May 19, 1963. Accompanying the president on his trip was Alabama senator Lister Hill, seen talking to the president on the stage as well as boarding the plane with him following his address. In his 1962 campaign for what he promised would be his last term in the Senate (he won his first Senate race in 1938), Lister promised funding for Redstone Arsenal as well as the Marshall Space Flight Center. (Courtesy of Alabama Department of Archives and History.)

5/19/63 - Armed Forces Day at Redstone Arsenal, Huntsville, Al

Gov. George Wallace visited the Huntsville Marshall Space Flight Center on June 8, 1965, during his first of four terms in office. In one picture, he is being shown a model of the static engine test stand by Dr. James Webb, NASA administrator (left), and Dr. Wernher von Braun (middle), Marshall Space Flight Center director. The other picture shows the three men engaged in a conversation. Governor Wallace would fight desegregation of Alabama universities. In 1968, Wallace ran for president as an independent, with Curtis LeMay, the general who prepared Strategic Air Command for its deterrent mission in the Cold War, as his running mate. (Courtesy of Alabama Department of Archives and History.)

Two famous astronauts from the original seven pilots selected for the Mercury program visited the space center in 1962. Alan Shepard (left) became the first American to go to space. John Glenn (center) achieved success as the first American to orbit the Earth. Both were pilots in the Mercury program, which selected the first American astronauts (or star travelers). The initial seven represented all services that had fixed-winged aircraft (Navy, Air Force, and Marines). Alan Shepard was a naval aviator, and John Glenn flew for the Marine Corps. (Courtesy of Alabama Department of Archives and History. Donated by Alabama Media Group. Photograph by Robert Adams, Birmingham News.)

Walt Disney, the famed creator of feature-length animated movies, visited the Marshall Space Flight Center in April 1965. Ten years prior, Wernher von Braun helped Disney create a television series, titled *Man in Space*, by serving as the technical director. Von Braun invited Disney to Huntsville to show him the progress on putting a man on the Moon. Here, von Braun is holding a model of his XR-1, a shuttle-like device that could take more humans into space and return. Von Braun died in 1977, four years before the launch of the actual space shuttle. (Courtesy of NASA.)

The Huntsville Saturn Static Test stand, built in 1956, tested the engines associated with several of the Redstone/Marshall programs to include Redstone, Jupiter, and Saturn. A Saturn booster is on the left in the stand. (Courtesy of Alabama Department of Archives and History.)

Two men oversee the assembly of the Saturn I at the Marshall Space Flight Center in Huntsville. The Saturn rocket was the principal vehicle for the Apollo program. The Saturn V would be used on the Apollo 11 mission that took the first Americans to the Moon. (Courtesy of Alabama Department of Archives and History. Donated by Alabama Media Group. Photograph by Anthony Falletta, Birmingham News.)

The rocket had to be moved to the static test stand for firing and testing. In this picture, an unidentified man is driving the Saturn V to the static stand. Due to the size of the rocket engines, it was a slow, arduous process. (Courtesy of Alabama Department of Archives and History. Donated by Alabama Media Group. Photograph by Tom Self, Birmingham News.)

The movement of the Saturn rockets to the test stand required a convoy-like procedure. Here, several cars and personnel supervise the movement of the rocket booster to the static stand. (Courtesy of Alabama Department of Archives and History. Donated by Alabama Media Group. Photograph by Tom Self, Birmingham News.)

After the movement of the Saturn rocket to the static test stand, preparations were made for the actual test. In one picture, Bernhard Tessmann (left) stands next to Wernher von Braun in front of a rocket booster ready for testing. Tessmann, like von Braun, worked on rocketry in Germany before coming the United States after World War II under Operation Paperclip. Tessmann was the deputy director of the test division at the Marshall Space Flight Center. (Courtesy of Alabama Department of Archives and History. Donated by Alabama Media Group. Photograph by Tom Self, Birmingham News.)

This picture gives an appreciation of the size of the Saturn V rocket and the engines that would drive the first stage. A one-tenth-scale model stands in front of the real Saturn booster, which could deliver over a million pounds of thrust. (Courtesy of Alabama Department of Archives and History.)

Model of Saturn Space Vehicle & "Real" Saturn Booster

Apollo/Saturn V Moon Rocket

A public display of the initial stage of the Saturn V rocket stands in the foreground with several of the successful Redstone and Marshall rocket programs in the background at the US Space and Rocket Center. Although it opened in 1970, von Braun had the idea for the center, intended to encourage public interest in rocketry, in the 1960s. (Courtesy of Alabama Department of Archives and History.)

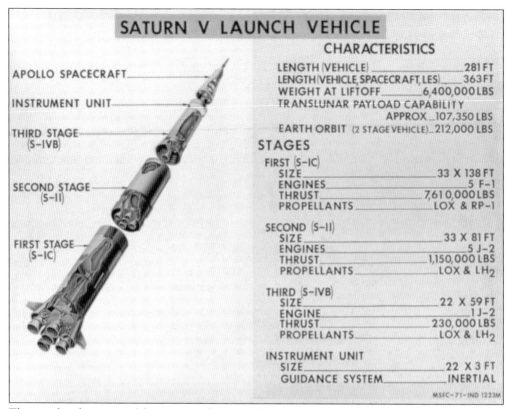

SATURN V LAUNCH VEHICLE

CHARACTERISTICS

LENGTH (VEHICLE) _____ 281 FT
LENGTH (VEHICLE, SPACECRAFT, LES) ____ 363 FT
WEIGHT AT LIFTOFF _____ 6,400,000 LBS
TRANSLUNAR PAYLOAD CAPABILITY
                                    APPROX ... 107,350 LBS
EARTH ORBIT (2 STAGE VEHICLE) ... 212,000 LBS

STAGES

FIRST (S-IC)
SIZE _____ 33 X 138 FT
ENGINES _____ 5 F-1
THRUST _____ 7,610,000 LBS
PROPELLANTS _____ LOX & RP-1

SECOND (S-II)
SIZE _____ 33 X 81 FT
ENGINES _____ 5 J-2
THRUST _____ 1,150,000 LBS
PROPELLANTS _____ LOX & LH$_2$

THIRD (S-IVB)
SIZE _____ 22 X 59 FT
ENGINE _____ 1 J-2
THRUST _____ 230,000 LBS
PROPELLANTS _____ LOX & LH$_2$

INSTRUMENT UNIT
SIZE _____ 22 X 3 FT
GUIDANCE SYSTEM _____ INERTIAL

MSFC-71-IND 1223M

Labels on diagram:
APOLLO SPACECRAFT
INSTRUMENT UNIT
THIRD STAGE (S-IVB)
SECOND STAGE (S-II)
FIRST STAGE (S-IC)

This graphic depiction of the Saturn V launch vehicle shows the three liquid-fueled stages. At the very top was the Apollo spacecraft, which consisted of a service module, a command module, and a lunar module. When the Apollo crew was free of Earth's gravity, they would stay in the service/command module until in orbit over the Moon. The lunar module would take two crewmembers to the Moon, with the third remaining in the service/command module. Once the Moon exploration was complete, the top part of the lunar module would rendezvous with the service/command module. Upon return to Earth, only the command module would re-enter the Earth's atmosphere and bring the astronauts back home. (Courtesy of NASA.)

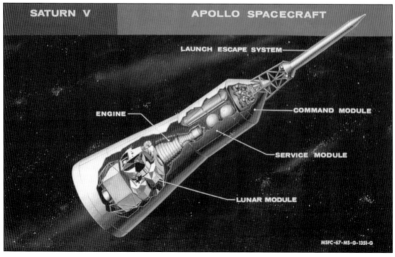

SATURN V   APOLLO SPACECRAFT
LAUNCH ESCAPE SYSTEM
ENGINE
COMMAND MODULE
SERVICE MODULE
LUNAR MODULE

MSFC-67-MS-G-1351-G

One way for NASA to simulate the weightlessness of space and the lower gravity of Moon was to train astronauts in water. A neutral buoyancy simulator was constructed at Huntsville in 1968. The tank at Huntsville was decommissioned in 1997. The idea behind the simulator was to use the neutral buoyancy environment of the water to help astronauts adapt to working in space. During its existence, the simulator helped astronauts develop and practice extra-vehicle activities (EVA). Johnson Space Center in Houston, Texas, would eventually construct a Weightless Environment Test Facility in the 1970s. Before that completion, Huntsville housed the only NASA test facility where astronauts could get used to the idea of being weightless. (Courtesy of NASA.)

Moon Crater at Night

Depicted here is the lunar module that would take the first two astronauts, Neil Armstrong and Edwin "Buzz" Aldrin, to the surface of the Moon. When the Moon exploration mission was complete, the top of the lunar module would separate and rendezvous with astronaut Michael Collins, who remained in the service/command module. (Courtesy of NASA.)

On July 20, 1969, astronaut Neil Armstrong descended the ladder from the lunar module and became the first human to set foot on the surface of the Moon. In an address to Congress in 1961, President Kennedy had established the national goal followed by his famous speech at Rice University in 1962. In less than a decade, America achieved Kennedy's objective, but Kennedy was assassinated in November 1963 and never got to see his goal become reality. (Courtesy of NASA.)

In downtown Huntsville, Alabama, Marshall Space Flight Center director Wernher von Braun is carried to the speaker's platform following the successful landing of Americans on the Moon. Von Braun would direct the space center until 1970. (Courtesy of Alabama Department of Archives and History.)

Marshall Space Flight Center director Wernher von Braun meets with John Goodloe, plant manager of the Thiokol Chemical Corporation facility at Redstone Arsenal, prior to touring the facility. Thiokol worked on solid rocket boosters and other government contracts from the Army. Thiokol would go on to develop the two solid rocket boosters, which would help launch the space shuttle in the 1980s and beyond. Unique to the design was the ability to recover the boosters for reuse. A problem with an O-ring in one of the boosters caused the shuttle disaster in 1986. (Courtesy of Alabama Department of Archives and History. Donated by Alabama Media Group. Photograph by Tom Self, Birmingham News.)

Following the success of the Apollo program, the United States attempted another first: putting the first space station in orbit. In 1971, the Soviet Union placed Salyut I in orbit. Using the same Saturn V rocket developed by the Marshall Space Flight Center, Skylab was put into orbit in 1973. The first mission was simply the space station. Three subsequent Skylab missions took Americans to the lab for increasing lengths of time (28, 60, and 84 days). Skylab astronauts conducted several experiments while in orbit including those submitted by students. After the last Skylab mission in 1964, Skylab's orbit would slowly decay until the space station burned up in the atmosphere on July 11, 1979. The accomplishments of the Skylab missions helped in the development of the International Space Station (ISS). (Courtesy of NASA.)

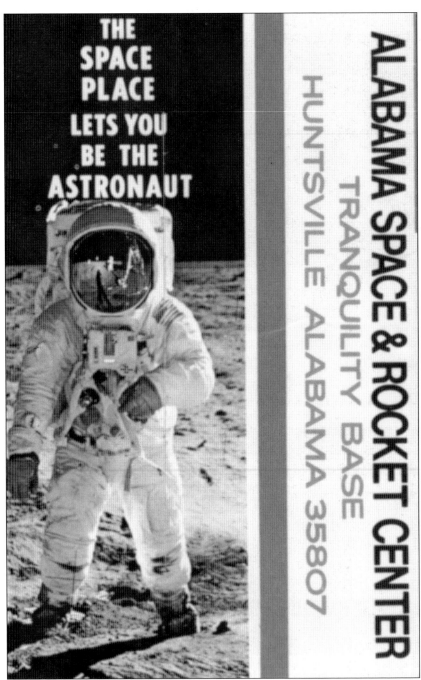

The success of the Mercury, Gemini, and Apollo programs increased the public's awareness of space exploration. The space program required a lot of talented people who understood rocketry, physics, and astrodynamics. While Operation Paperclip provided some of the first talented people, the United States needed young Americans to enter the science, technology, engineering, and math fields. Determined and focused efforts were made to attract young people to a career in space by offering camps and experiences mimicking space flight. (Courtesy of Alabama Department of Archives and History.)

Besides the Huntsville US Space and Rocket Center, NASA opened a Space Camp in 1982 as a way to attract young people to the field of space. In one picture, camp attendees sit at a control panel during a session. Camp goers also had the chance to shoot rockets. The idea for the camp came from Wernher von Braun, who noticed the fascination children had with the rockets on display at the Space and Rocket Center. Since opening its doors, close to 900,000 students have gone through the camp. (Courtesy of Alabama Department of Archives and History.)

EARTH'S LARGEST SPACE EXIBIT

Earth's Largest Space Exhibit

Huntsville, situated in the northeast part of Alabama, has become "rocket town." What began as a chemical munitions and storage place in World War II was transformed into the Army's Redstone Arsenal. Redstone led the way for the Army's ballistic missile program. Ballistic missiles would become a central feature in the Cold War, as would the race for space. The Marshall Space Flight Center produced the rockets necessary to achieve President Kennedy's vision in well under a decade. Both places were key to the United States winning the space race and the Cold War. (Courtesy of Alabama Department of Archives and History.)

Three

THE HOME FRONT FIGHT
THE CIVIL RIGHTS MOVEMENT

The civil rights movement deserves a place in a discussion on the Cold War because of the US strategy. The United States wanted to extol the virtues of democracy and its superiority over communism as a form of government. As the country attempted to promote democracy on a global scale and grow its influence in the world, America had a problem at home. Not everyone was fully participating in the democracy about which the United States boasted. Post-Reconstruction Jim Crow laws, segregation (the idea of separate but equal), and voting rights abuses had limited the ability of a significant minority to fully realize the "more perfect Union" the Constitution advocated.

National leaders wanted to communicate an image of democracy and equality abroad, but certain states within the country were still dealing with segregation and inequality. Alabama became a focal point in the civil rights movement. From Birmingham to Montgomery, Tuscaloosa to Gadsden, Dr. Martin Luther King Jr.'s strategy of nonviolent disobedience was on full display. The pictures will show a few of the tactics used during the civil rights movement. Marches were an obvious way to draw attention to the cause. Sit-ins, started by a group of college students in North Carolina, were a way to highlight the segregation policies that allowed one seating section for Whites and another for Blacks. Freedom riding was another prominent tactic in the movement. Black, and sometimes White, passengers would ride interstate travel buses (and even airplanes) to protest segregation on interstate transportation.

This chapter also highlights another important aspect of the civil rights movement: the desegregation of public universities. The post-Reconstruction policy was separate but equal education for Whites and Blacks. In 1954, the Supreme Court unanimously ruled that the policy of separate but equal violated the Constitution. Alabama public universities would welcome Black students on their campuses, but not without some controversy.

The following pages show in pictures how the civil rights movement played out in Alabama. There is no separating the civil rights movement and the Cold War. National leaders in Washington, DC, used the full power of the federal government to enforce court decisions and the law. These actions were done to show the world that equality and democracy were on full display in America, which held hope for a better form of government than its communist adversary.

Autherine Lucy and Arthur Shores read Lucy's letter of admission to the University of Alabama. Following the Supreme Court ruling on Brown vs. Board of Education, Shores argued before the Supreme Court, in Lucy v. Adams, that the University of Alabama could not deny admission strictly based on race. Shores won his court case, and Lucy started classes in February 1956. There were several protests to her attendance, some of which turned violent. After attending classes for three days, the university expelled her for her own safety following the protests. In 2022, the University of Alabama dedicated the College of Education building in her honor. (Courtesy of Alabama Department of Archives and History. Donated by Alabama Media Group. Photograph by Ed Jones, Birmingham News.)

These pictures highlight some of the demonstrations that followed Autherine Lucy's admission to and attendance at the University of Alabama. In one picture, students are raising Confederate flags at an anti-integration rally in Tuscaloosa. The other picture shows students performing a cross burning. These protests influenced the university's decision to expel Lucy. (Courtesy of Alabama Department of Archives and History. Donated by Alabama Media Group. Unidentified photographer, Birmingham News.)

Alabama universities were integrated in 1963. On June 13, 1963, Dave Mack McGlathery became the first Black student to attend the University of Alabama in Huntsville. (Courtesy of the Alabama Department of Archives and History.)

Dave Mack McGlathery, the first Black student at the University of Alabama in Huntsville, makes his way to his first class. McGlathery was a mathematician at the Marshall Space Flight Center in Huntsville and enrolled for graduate study. (Courtesy of the Alabama Department of Archives and History.)

US deputy attorney general Nicholas Katzenbach (left) oversaw Dave Mack McGlathery's first day on the campus of University of Alabama at Huntsville. Here, he speaks with two unidentified men, one of whom (on the right) appears to be a public safety officer. (Courtesy of the Alabama Department of Archives and History.)

In June 1963, Vivian Malone and James Hood entered the University of Alabama in Tuscaloosa. It had been seven years since Autherine Lucy had first attended the university. Malone and Hood are pictured outside Foster Auditorium on the campus. (Courtesy of the Alabama Department of Archives and History.)

Vivian Malone leaves Foster Auditorium after registering for classes at the University of Alabama. Born in Mobile, Alabama, in 1942, Malone was the fourth of eight children. Prior to enrolling in the University of Alabama, Malone attended Alabama Agricultural and Mechanical University, a Black college in Alabama. After two years at the university, Malone graduated with a bachelor's of arts degree in business management and became the first Black student to graduate from the university. Following graduation, no one in Alabama offered Malone a job. She eventually took a job in Washington, DC, where worked as a researcher for the civil rights division at the US Department of Justice. (Courtesy of the Alabama Department of Archives and History.)

On June 11, 1963, Gov. George Wallace makes a "stand in the schoolhouse door" in an effort to prevent the desegregation of the University of Alabama. When running for governor of Alabama, Wallace ran on the promise of "Segregation Now, Segregation Tomorrow, Segregation Forever." Addressing the governor is US deputy attorney general Nicholas Katzenbach. Wallace was unsuccessful in his attempt to prevent Vivian Malone and James Hood from registering. Although Wallace brought out the National Guard (which reports to the governor) to help enforce his stance, President Kennedy "federalized" the National Guard (which means the troops now report to the president). The now federalized commander of the guard, Gen. Henry Graham, ordered Wallace to step aside. (Courtesy of Alabama Department of Archives and History. Donated by Alabama Media Group. Photograph by Robert Adams, Birmingham News.)

Governor Wallace sits in a highway patrol car on the day he attempted to "stand in the door" and prevent the desegregation of the University of Alabama. President Kennedy and Wallace were both Democrats, but Wallace felt Northern Democrats had abandoned the South; he would run unsuccessfully for president in 1968. (Courtesy of Alabama Department of Archives and History.)

Not until 1967 did the University of Alabama football program accept its first Black player. Inspired by Alabama's 1966 undefeated season, Dock Rone walked on in 1967 to play for Coach "Bear" Bryant. (Courtesy of Alabama Department of Archives and History. Donated by Alabama Media Group. Photograph by Jerry Moulder, Birmingham News.)

The desegregation of schools was only one battle in the civil rights movement. Rosa Parks's refusal to sit in "the back of the bus" opened another front in the battle for equality. Although other Blacks had previously refused to sit in the "Blacks only" section of Montgomery buses, organizers thought Parks was the best person to see the cause go through the court system. Seated next to Parks in the picture is Dr. Martin Luther King Jr. Dr. King, a Morehouse College, Crozer Theological Seminary, and Boston University (PhD) graduate, came to Montgomery in 1954 to pastor the Dexter Baptist Church. He became a prominent leader in the civil rights movement. As a new resident of Montgomery, he was unencumbered by the state's and city's political machine. Parks's resistance eventually led to a court decision that ruled bus segregation illegal. (Courtesy of National Archives, National Archives record ID: 306-PSD-65-1882 [Box 93].)

Pastor Fred Shuttlesworth of Bethel Baptist Church in Birmingham was another prominent figure in the civil rights movement. With Dr. King and other activists, Shuttlesworth founded the Southern Christian Leadership Conference (SCLC), a civil rights organization based in Atlanta, Georgia. Rosa Parks's refusal to sit in the Blacks-only section of a Montgomery bus led to a Supreme Court ruling in December 1956 that bus segregation was illegal. Shuttlesworth organized riders to board Birmingham buses in order to enforce the high court's ruling. (Courtesy of Alabama Department of Archives and History. Donated by Alabama Media Group. Photograph by Tommy Hill and Sally Samuel, Birmingham News.)

Churches became a focal point for organizing and motivating Blacks to continue the fight for equality. Here, Pastor Fred Shuttlesworth addresses his congregation on the need to fight for enforcement of the court's ruling on desegregating buses. (Courtesy of Alabama Department of Archives and History. Donated by Alabama Media Group. Photograph by Al Stanton and Samuel, Birmingham News.)

Members of the Bethel Baptist Church listen to Pastor Shuttlesworth encouraging the congregation to continue nonviolent attempts to desegregate buses. Shuttlesworth's campaign to desegregate the Birmingham buses did lead to attempts on his life, including the placement of dynamite at his house. (Courtesy of Alabama Department of Archives and History. Donated by Alabama Media Group. Photograph by Al Stanton and Samuel, Birmingham News.)

Fred Shuttlesworth's attempt to desegregate Birmingham buses resulted in arrests and threats to assembled riders. Shuttlesworth addressed the congregation after the initial attempt to desegregate the buses. Prior to the effort, Rev. Fred Shuttlesworth issued a statement saying that unless buses were desegregated in next six days, Blacks would attempt to do it themselves. Shuttlesworth efforts did not stop with buses. In 1957, Shuttlesworth and his wife, Ruby Keeler Shuttlesworth, attempted to enroll their kids in a White-only school only to be beaten so severely that Shuttlesworth had to drive his wife and himself to a hospital for treatment. One of his assailants, Bobby Frank Cherry, would later participate in the bombing of the Sixteenth Street Church. (Courtesy of Alabama Department of Archives and History. Donated by Alabama Media Group. Photograph by Al Stanton and Samuel, Birmingham News.)

In addition to desegregating schools and buses, the civil rights movement sought to desegregate transportation hubs as well. "Freedom Riders" were Black and White riders who volunteered to ride interstate commerce (mostly buses but airplanes as well) to seek enforcement of the court ruling that segregation was illegal. In the first picture, police officers are covering the windshield of a Greyhound bus to hide freedom riders at the terminal in Birmingham, Alabama. The other picture shows the aftermath of an attack on a bus near Anniston, Alabama. (Above, courtesy of Alabama Department of Archives and History. Donated by Alabama Media Group. Photograph by Robert Adams and Norman Dean, Birmingham News; below, courtesy of Alabama Department of Archives and History. Donated by Alabama Media Group. Photograph by Hornsby, Birmingham News.)

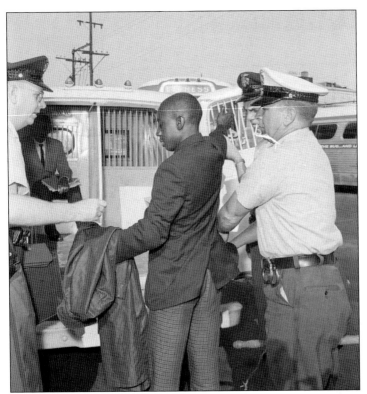

In this image, Freedom Rider Charles Butler is arrested by local police. This occurred at the Greyhound bus terminal in Birmingham, Alabama. (Courtesy of Alabama Department of Archives and History. Donated by Alabama Media Group. Photograph by Robert Adams and Norman Dean, Birmingham News.)

The National Guard would be called out to help protect buses with Freedom Riders. Here, the National Guard is protecting a group of riders leaving Montgomery, Alabama, for Jackson, Mississippi. (Courtesy of Alabama Department of Archives and History. Donated by Alabama Media Group. Photograph by Norman Dean, Birmingham News.)

Sit-ins were another nonviolent civil disobedience tactic employed during the civil rights movement. The tactic and the focus of the demonstrations were to desegregate lunch counters where Blacks had to sit in one area and Whites in another. In 1960, in Greensboro, North Carolina, a group of college students was among the first to sit at Whites-only lunch counters. The students would go on to form the Student Nonviolent Coordinating Committee (SNCC). Ella Baker, while executive secretary of SCLC, spearheaded the formation of SNCC. Baker was one of few women to help start and organize a civil rights organization. The North Carolina effort to desegregate lunch counters soon spread to other Southern states. Here, sit-in protestors are escorted out of a downtown Birmingham drugstore. (Courtesy of Alabama Department of Archives and History. Donated by Alabama Media Group. Photograph by Ed Jones, Birmingham News.)

In April 1963, Birmingham, Alabama, became the focal point of the civil rights movement. Protests, demonstrations, and sit-ins in Birmingham would bring attention to the city's various segregation policies. The civil rights movement picked Birmingham as a focus of its campaign because the city was deeply segregated. Furthermore, 40 percent of the city's resident were Black, but there were no Black police officers, firefighters, or bus drivers. Tensions between the races had gotten so bad with several unsolved bombings in Black areas of town that the city earned the name "Bombingham." When the city's law enforcement responded to the protests by turning water hoses on participants, the images were captured by media as well as television and brought national attention to the movement. (Courtesy of Alabama Department of Archives and History. Donated by Alabama Media Group. Photograph by Ed Jones and Robert Adams, Birmingham News.)

Pastor Fred Shuttlesworth (pictured above) along with other protestors confront a Birmingham police officer. Below, a large contingent of protestors are arrested and put into a police transport. One objective civil rights leaders had for the Birmingham protest was to get as many people jailed as possible (to include children) and fill up the city jails. By having a significant number of people arrested, the civil rights leaders felt they would demonstrate the number of people who would fight for equality. (Courtesy of Alabama Department of Archives and History. Donated by Alabama Media Group. Photograph by Ed Jones and Robert Adams, Birmingham News.)

Perhaps no person better represents Birmingham's resistance to Project C (organizers nicknamed the Birmingham protest Project C for Confrontation) than Eugene "Bull" Connor. In April 1963, Connor, a strict segregationist, had just lost the mayoral race against a more moderate candidate. At the time, he was serving as the commissioner of public safety for the city of Birmingham. Connor had previously been a sports announcer and earned the "Bull" nickname because of his booming voice. His direction to local law enforcement to turn water hoses and dogs on protestors was captured by national media and earned President Kennedy's attention. In one picture, Connor and Gov. John Patterson are with an unidentified young boy at the opening of Eastwood Mall in Birmingham in 1960. In the other picture, Connor watches demonstrators with an unidentified law enforcement officer. (Above, courtesy of Alabama Department of Archives and History; below, courtesy of Alabama Department of Archives and History. Donated by Alabama Media Group. Photograph by Norman Dean and Lou Isaacson, Birmingham News.)

Birmingham was not the only place where protestors took to the streets to draw attention to segregation practices by Alabama businesses. In the picture above, protestors take to the sidewalks of Gadsden, Alabama, in solidarity with the Birmingham protestors. (Courtesy of Alabama Department of Archives and History. Donated by Alabama Media Group. Photograph by Anthony Falletta, Birmingham News.)

Dr. Martin Luther King Jr. visited Gadsden as protestors took to the street. Here, Dr. King addresses a congregation at a local Gadsden church. (Courtesy of Alabama Department of Archives and History. Donated by Alabama Media Group. Photograph by Ed Jones, Birmingham News.)

Black churches in Alabama were meeting places where pastors rallied their congregations to the civil rights cause and organized nonviolent tactics and actions. That meant Black churches were also targets of those opposed to desegregation. Five months after the Birmingham protests, on September 15, 1963, four members of the Ku Klux Klan planted dynamite with a timing device under the Sixteenth Street Church. When the dynamite exploded, the blast tore through the church and killed four girls—Addie Mae Collins, Cynthia Wesley, Carole Robertson, and Carol Denise McNair—who were in the church basement. The picture above shows the damage done to the church from the bombing. At left, victims arrive at University Hospital in Birmingham. (Above, courtesy of Alabama Department of Archives and History. Donated by Alabama Media Group. Photograph by Tom Self, Birmingham News; left, courtesy of Alabama Department of Archives and History. Donated by Alabama Media Group. Photograph by Lou Isaacson, Birmingham News.)

The blast at the Sixteenth Street Church was so powerful that it damaged or destroyed cars parked nearby. The effect of the blast caused damage to houses and windows up to two blocks away. The church was likely picked as a target because of its proximity to Birmingham's commercial district and city hall. Although a place people gathered to worship, the church also functioned as a place for meeting for social activities as well as planning civil rights meetings and rallies. In fact, several of the Project C protestors started their march to downtown from the church. (Courtesy of Alabama Department of Archives and History. Donated by Alabama Media Group. Photograph by Anthony Falletta, Birmingham News.)

A woman talks to a law enforcement officer outside the site of the blast. The Federal Bureau of Investigation (FBI) identified four members of the Ku Klux Klan—Robert E. Chambliss, Bobby Frank Cherry, Herman Frank Cash, and Thomas E. Blanton Jr.—as suspects. Although suspected of the crime, reluctant witnesses and insufficient evidence delayed prosecution until the 1970s. Elected in 1970, Alabama attorney general Robert Baxley took up the "cold case" against Chambliss and won a conviction in 1977. Chambliss was sentenced to life in jail. In the 1990s, the FBI opened cases against Blanton and Cherry (Cash died in 1994). On May 16, 2000, an Alabama grand jury indicted Blanton and Cherry. Cherry was initially ruled incompetent to stand trial due to dementia, but Blanton was eventually convicted and sentenced to life in jail. A judge later determined Cherry competent to stand trial, which resulted in a conviction and life sentence as well. (Courtesy of Alabama Department of Archives and History. Donated by Alabama Media Group. Photograph by Vernon Merritt, Birmingham News)

When it comes to the civil rights movement, there may be no more famous church in Alabama than the Dexter Avenue Baptist Church in downtown Montgomery. Dr. Martin Luther King Jr. served as pastor there from 1954 until 1960. It is the site where the Montgomery boycott and the effort to desegregate buses began. In the picture above, congregation members and activists are leaving the church presumably on a march to the capitol building (in Montgomery) to protest segregation throughout the state. (Courtesy of Alabama Department of Archives and History. Donated by Alabama Media Group. Photograph by Tom Self, Birmingham News.)

In response to the death of a Black protestor trying to fight for voting rights, Southern Christian Leadership Conference organizer James Bevel wanted a series of marches to highlight the need for voting reform. Three marches were planned from Selma to the state capitol in Montgomery. The first march took place on March 7, 1965, otherwise known as "Bloody Sunday," when state troopers attacked protestors with clubs and tear gas. One protestor, Amelia Boynton, was captured by media lying unconscious on the Edmund Pettus Bridge. The events caught the attention of Pres. Lyndon Johnson, who federalized the Alabama National Guard to protect protestors on their third march on March 21, 1965. Above, a woman leads a group of protestors along Highway 80 to Montgomery. Below shows Dr. Martin Luther King Jr., Coretta Scott King, Southern Christian Leadership Conference organizer James Bevel, and others on the Selma march. (Above, courtesy of Alabama Department of Archives and History. Donated by Alabama Media Group. Photograph by Spider Martin, Birmingham News; below, courtesy of Alabama Department of Archives and History.)

This picture shows Selma marchers arriving in the Alabama capital city of Montgomery. The marchers walked an average of 10 miles a day. They arrived in Montgomery on March 24, the day before the formally organized capitol building protest was to occur. (Courtesy of Alabama Department of Archives and History.)

While Montgomery was a focal point in the civil rights movement, it was also a place where the Catholic church sought to bring education to Black children. Pictured here are children praying with nuns at the Nazareth Catholic Mission in Montgomery, Alabama. (Courtesy of Alabama Department of Archives and History.)

The Cold War would place a premium on Americans educated in hard sciences as it sought to build ballistic missiles and extend America's space exploration. Here, children at the Nazareth Catholic Church are solving arithmetic problems. (Courtesy of Alabama Department of Archives and History.)

A female student makes a presentation to her fellow classmates at the Nazareth Catholic Church in Montgomery. Today, the school is closed. (Courtesy of Alabama Department of Archives and History.)

Four

THE MILITARY FRONT
PROXY WARS AND HELICOPTERS

Many call the period between 1946 and 1991 the Cold War because the two superpowers in the world—the United States and the Soviet Union—never actually engaged in head-to-head combat. Despite the United States having a nuclear arsenal that reached a peak of close to 32,000 nuclear weapons, with the Soviet Union mirroring those numbers, the two nations never engaged in all-out war. That does not mean the two nations never engaged in combat during this period. Instead of direct engagement, the struggle between communism and democracy played out through proxy wars, mostly in East and Southeast Asia.

Following World War II, the country of Korea was divided along the 38th parallel into two sovereign states, North Korea and South Korea. North Korea aligned itself with China and the Soviet Union, while South Korea affiliated itself with the United States. In June 1950, North Korean forces supplied by China and the Soviet Union invaded South Korea. The United States came to South Korea's aid but would need to draft manpower to fend off the communist forces. A famous Alabama sports hero would be among the many called to serve in the US military.

A decade later, a similar situation would play out in Vietnam when a communist-backed North Vietnam aimed to force unification with a US-backed South Vietnam. Since Korea, however, the Army had been working on a new tactic for these proxy, insurgent wars. Helicopters would be used to rapidly infiltrate troops into areas. An Army base in southern Alabama, Fort Rucker, would be the initial training ground for these helicopter pilots. The Vietnam War would also produce a significant number of refugees who sought to flee the North's communist regime. Alabama would be a welcome sight to some of these refugees fleeing communism.

During the Cold War, women found increasing opportunities to serve in the US military. Initially named the Women's Army Auxiliary Corps, the women's corps in the Army was later changed to the Women's Army Corps and headquartered at Fort McClellan in Aniston, Alabama. Toward the end of the 1970s, the Women's Army Corps was no longer required, as women were allowed to serve alongside men in the US military.

While nuclear-armed bombers and missiles kept the Cold War from turning "hot," others in Alabama prepared, trained, and fought in small wars that aimed to contain the spread of communism.

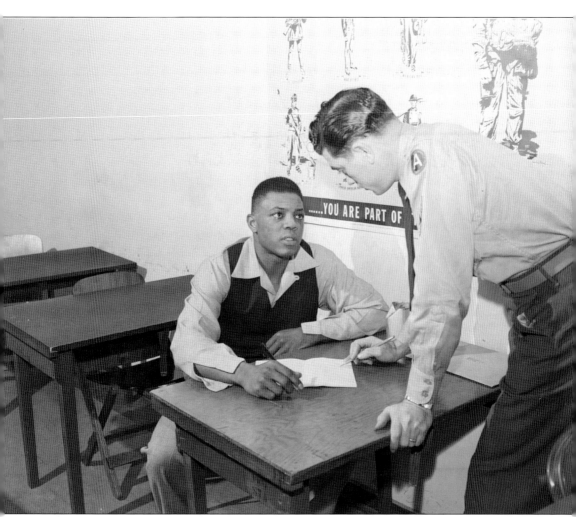

The need for manpower for the Korean War required a draft. Here, Westfield, Alabama, native Willie Mays signs his US Army draft paperwork in 1952. The future hall of fame major league baseball player had just been named rookie of the year following his initial season with the New York (later the San Francisco) Giants. After World War II, the US military significantly downsized. Mays spent his time in the Army stateside at Fort Eustis, Virginia, where he played baseball for the Army. Following his return to baseball in 1954, Mays helped the Giants win the World Series. (Courtesy of Alabama Department of Archives and History. Donated by Alabama Media Group. Photograph by Ed Jones, Birmingham News.)

Initially stood up to train pilots for the Army during World War II, Craig Air Force Base would see increased action during the Korean War. The Air Force (a newly independent service since 1947) needed to produce pilots that would have the skills necessary to fly jet aircraft. The Korean War would not only be the first war for newly independent Air Force, but it would also be the first to feature jet aircraft on both sides of the conflict. (Courtesy of Alabama Department of Archives and History. Donated by Alabama Media Group. Photograph by Frank Sikora, Birmingham News.)

Jet engines, like the one being highlighted by this National Guard airman at Garrett Coliseum during the 1954 South Alabama Fair, would become the main form of propulsion for military and commercial aircraft following World War II. A jet engine functions differently than a propeller-driven aircraft. A propeller could be attached to the crankshaft of a standard piston driven engine to pull the aircraft through the air. Jet engines use a series of fans to compress the incoming air. Fuel is then added, and a spark provided to ignite the compressed air. As the heated air leaves the combustion chamber, it propels the aircraft forward. This jet engine design allowed aircraft to fly higher and faster than previous propeller-driven aircraft. (Courtesy of Alabama Department of Archives and History.)

Developing and fielding jet aircraft would be the main focus of the newly independent Air Force. Here, Alabama governor John Patterson sits in a F-84F being instructed by an Air Force officer. Republic F-84F "Thunderstreaks" would be stationed in Alabama and flown by the Alabama Air National Guard. (Courtesy of Alabama Department of Archives and History.)

Named for the first female senator to represent Alabama, Dixie Bibb Graves, Fort Dixie Armory was another Alabama site that recruited and fielded National Guard troops such as these. This came at a time when the nation needed additional manpower. (Courtesy of Alabama Department of Archives and History.)

Disclaimer: This book will refer to Fort Rucker for historical context. The fort was named for a Confederate colonel and per direction of the 2021 National Defense Authorization Act and the secretary of defense, in 2023 the name was changed to Fort Novosel. Michael Novosel was an Enterprise, Alabama, native who won the Medal of Honor for his heroics while a helicopter pilot in the Vietnam War. The Army used Fort Rucker for infantry training, but it eventually became home to the Army Aviation School. (Courtesy of Alabama Department of Archives and History.)

Fort Rucker began as "Camp Rucker" in World War II and was used for infantry training. After the war, the fort largely remained inactive until the Korean War. The need for more training and manpower saw the fort reopened for basic training. (Courtesy of Alabama Department of Archives and History.)

During the Korean War, infantry troops would train at Camp Rucker before being sent as replacements to Central Asia. Following the war, the Army wanted to develop more organic close air support to support its troops (in the form of armed helicopters). Additionally, the Army wanted to rapidly transport troops to the battle using its own helicopters. The increased need for helicopters, and pilots to fly them, made Fort Rucker the primary place for helicopter training in the US Army. (Courtesy of Alabama Department of Archives and History.)

An Army trooper refuels a Bell H-13 Sioux helicopter at Fort Rucker. Rotary aircraft were primarily used in the Korean War for observation, reconnaissance of enemy positions, and medical evacuation of wounded troops. (Courtesy of Alabama Department of Archives and History. Donated by Alabama Media Group. Photograph by Ed Jones, Birmingham News.)

The H-13 would also be used by the Army during the Vietnam War for observation. As the Army increased the roles and missions for the helicopter, it would pursue enclosed cockpits, armaments, and additional specialties for its helicopter fleet. (Courtesy of Alabama Department of Archives and History. Donated by Alabama Media Group. Photograph by Ed Jones, Birmingham News.)

The Army firmly established Fort Rucker as the Army Aviation Center in 1955. While the Air Force had previously trained helicopter pilots, in 1956, the Department of Defense made the decision to allow the Army to train its own pilots. The Army saw a need for a more than an observation role for its helicopters, and Fort Rucker is where the Army began testing various forms of armament. (Courtesy of Alabama Department of Archives and History. Donated by Alabama Media Group. Photograph by Ed Jones, Birmingham News.)

Pictured here at Fort Rucker is one of the earliest versions of a tandem rotor helicopter. The US Army flew the H-21 Shawnee up to and throughout the Vietnam War. Eventually, the Army would equip the helicopter with door guns. Its unique design earned it the nickname "the flying banana." (Courtesy of Alabama Department of Archives and History. Donated by Alabama Media Group. Photograph by Ed Jones, Birmingham News.)

A helicopter pilot flies over the fort for training. While the Air Force only sent commissioned officers to pilot training, the bulk of Army helicopter pilots were warrant officers. The warrant officer rank indicates a highly skilled, single-track specialty officer who ranks above all enlisted ranks but below those of commissioned officers. (Courtesy of Alabama Department of Archives and History. Donated by Alabama Media Group. Photograph by Ed Jones, Birmingham News.)

When the US Army set up its Army Aviation Center at Fort Rucker, it placed the US Army post in Dale County. Several surrounding cities, including Ozark, Enterprise, and Daleville, service the base. (Courtesy of Alabama Department of Archives and History. Donated by Alabama Media Group. Photograph by Ed Jones, Birmingham News.)

The Army used the H-19 Chickasaw, pictured above, as its first unarmed transport helicopter. Engine placement was different in the H-19. The crew actually sat above the engine, which was located in front of the main cabin. Placement of the engine was done to make it to maintain proper weight and balance since the powerplant was close to the aircraft's center of gravity. The Army began exploring the idea of an air mobility missions for the Army in the Korean War. It was not until the Vietnam War and the battle of Ia Drang Valley (the account of which is told in the book *We Were Soldiers Once . . . and Young: Ia Drang–The Battle That Changed the War in Vietnam*) where the Army's true air mobility mission would be tested in combat. (Courtesy of Alabama Department of Archives and History. Donated by Alabama Media Group. Photograph by Ed Jones, Birmingham News.)

A soldier at Fort Rucker holds a belt of 40-milliliter explosive shells in front of a helicopter. The Army felt its troops suffered from a lack of air support in the Korean War. Therefore, the service sought to develop an organic capability to support its troops with air delivered munitions in battle. Armed helicopters offered the Army a solution. At Fort Rucker, armaments would be added to helicopter frames. Although helicopters would initially have machine guns and explosive shells, the Army would eventually add rockets and anti-tank missiles. (Courtesy of Alabama Department of Archives and History. Donated by Alabama Media Group. Photograph by Ed Jones, Birmingham News.)

"Huey" Helicopter   Ft. Rucker, Alabama

The Army started to develop the Bell UH-1 Iroquois, otherwise known as the Huey, in the early 1950s. Since it came online after the Korean War, its first use in combat was in the Vietnam War. While medical evacuation of the wounded and cargo transport were some of its primary missions, air assault or transporting troops to the battle zone were other vital missions. Eventually, the Army would arm the Huey with rockets, grenade launchers, and guns. (Courtesy of Alabama Department of Archives and History.)

AH-1G "Cobra" Helicopter   Fort Rucker, Alabama

The Cobra helicopter pictured above is the Bell AH-1. It came into service primarily to provide dedicated fires (rockets, guns, and so on) to Army infantry on the ground. This helicopter, a modification of the H-1, became operational in 1967 and was quickly sent to the Vietnam theater. Besides Vietnam, it would see service in Grenada (1984) and Operation Desert Storm (1990–1991). (Courtesy of Alabama Department of Archives and History.)

William "Bill" Wood Jr. spent a career of service to the Air Force and to the cause of the Cold War. Wood was born in February 1935 in Alexander City, Alabama. He graduated from Mellow Valley High School in 1952, and he attended Alabama Polytechnic Institute (later named Auburn University), earning a degree in aeronautical engineering. Following graduation, he entered the US Air Force, where he would complete pilot training. He would train other pilots to fly but would deploy to Vietnam as a forward air controller. (Courtesy of Alabama Department of Archives and History.)

Lieutenant Wood attended basic flight instructor training at Craig Air Force Base in Selma. He graduated from the training in 1959. His graduating class is pictured here. (Courtesy of Alabama Department of Archives and History.)

Lieutenant Wood initially taught others how to fly. Pictured here is Wood in front of the T-33A Shooting Star, a tandem-seated jet trainer. The trainer came from the F-80 fighter, which was the first jet aircraft used by the United States in combat (first World War II and then Korea). (Courtesy of Alabama Department of Archives and History.)

In December 1966, Capt. Bill Wood deployed out of California to South Vietnam for a one-year tour. His mission would be to fly forward air control missions in order to direct other planes toward their target. This picture depicts his departure. (Courtesy of Alabama Department of Archives and History.)

During his one-year tour in Vietnam, Captain Wood was promoted to major just prior to his return in 1967. Wood took this picture of Bien Hoa Air Base, which was a major air base that all US military aircraft used during the Vietnam War. (Courtesy of Alabama Department of Archives and History.)

While serving in Vietnam, Major Wood was able to visit Bangkok, Thailand. He took this picture of the Grand Palace in Bangkok during his tour. Although only one building is pictured, the Grand Palace is actually a complex of multiple buildings. Construction on the palace began in 1782. Since that time, it has served as the central residence of the Kings of Siam (later Thailand). During the Vietnam War, Thailand became concerned about the ongoing war in Vietnam. Eventually, the government of Thailand allowed up to 50,000 military personnel to be stationed in Thailand. Thailand itself would eventually send troops to help South Vietnam in its fight against the communist forces of North Vietnam. (Courtesy of Alabama Department of Archives and History.)

Upon returning from Vietnam, newly promoted Maj. Bill Wood would head to Houston, Texas, to serve in NASA's Office of Lunar Surface Operations prior to and through the Apollo 11 mission to the Moon. Wood's time in that office was spent on extravehicular activity, which could be outside the vehicle in space or outside the vehicle on the surface of another body. In appreciation for his efforts, the Apollo 11 crew sent him a signed note of thanks. Additionally, the US Air Force would give Wood a Meritorious Service Medal. Wood would go on to help Apollo 14 with its mission preparation. Apollo 14 was the first Moon landing mission to venture into the lunar highlands. (Courtesy of Alabama Department of Archives and History.)

The chief of staff of the Army, Gen. Matthew Ridgway visited Fort McClellan in 1954 to dedicate the permanent home of the Women's Army Corps (WAC). In World War II, the United States started the Women's Army Auxiliary Corps (WAAC) in 1942. Since women in the WAAC technically had no military status, the Women's Army Corps took its place becoming part of the active Army in 1943. When the Korean War broke out, women were also needed in increased numbers. In 1951, the Army established a permanent home for the WAC was established at Fort McClellan near Anniston, Alabama. (Courtesy of Alabama Department of Archives and History. Donated by Alabama Media Group. Photograph by Tommy Hill, Birmingham News.)

Gen. Matthew Ridgway, a World War II veteran who led operations in Italy and the landing in Normandy, performed the dedication of the WAC center in 1954. During Korea, Ridgway took command of 8th Army (1950) and is largely credited with turning the tide of the war effort. Ridgway would serve as supreme allied commander Europe (1952) and, eventually, became the Army's chief of staff in 1953. This was his position when he conducted the dedication. Creating the WAC center provided women basic training as well as training in stenography, clerk-typist, stenography, and personnel specialist. (Courtesy of Alabama Department of Archives and History. Donated by Alabama Media Group. Photograph by Tommy Hill, Birmingham News.)

Two Women's Army Corps members inspect a large cooking pot on post at Fort McClellan. The WAC center at Fort McClellan served as a training post for women entering the corps. (Courtesy of Alabama Department of Archives and History. Donated by Alabama Media Group. Photograph by Norman Dean, Birmingham News.)

During the dedication of the post at Fort McClellan, WAC members served alongside active-duty males. Pictured here are military police keeping guard during the ceremony. (Courtesy of Alabama Department of Archives and History. Donated by Alabama Media Group. Photograph by Tommy Hill, Birmingham News.)

The post at Fort McClellan had active-duty as well as reservist WACs. Here, WAC reservists in 1955 participate in a marchout during their two-week active-duty training. (Courtesy of Alabama Department of Archives and History.)

Training at the WAC center went beyond simple clerical duties. WAC members also practiced with rifles during their training. (Courtesy of Alabama Department of Archives and History. Donated by Alabama Media Group. Photograph by Charles Nix, Birmingham News.)

Prior to the arrival of the Women's Army Corps, Fort McClellan was the Army's chemical school. With the increased missions and demands of the war in Vietnam, the Army opened a training center at the post. In 1966, the Army activated the Advanced Individual Training Infantry Brigade. Fort McClellan would become the only Army installation with three major commands. During the 1960s, Fort McClellan would train more than 30,000 troops for service in Vietnam. As the war came to a close, the Training Infantry Brigade was deactivated in 1970. Pictured here are soldiers training in the Army's new air assault/air mobility mission. (Courtesy of Alabama Department of Archives and History. Donated by Alabama Media Group. Photograph by Robert Adams, Birmingham News.)

At the Army Training Center at Fort McClellan, soldiers learned the skills necessary for fighting the Cold War's proxy wars. Soldiers would practice air assault/air mobility to rapidly deploy to battles and bring maneuver back to the battlefield. (Courtesy of Alabama Department of Archives and History. Donated by Alabama Media Group. Photograph by Robert Adams, Birmingham News.)

The Vietnam War was a complicated conflict. In addition to fighting the conventional North Vietnamese Army, US troops had to fight the insurgent Viet Cong forces attempting to infiltrate South Vietnam. At Fort McClellan, deploying soldiers practice insurgent techniques with soldiers role-playing as the Vietnam populace. (Courtesy of Alabama Department of Archives and History. Donated by Alabama Media Group. Photograph by Robert Adams, Birmingham News.)

Alabama native John Caldwell served as a mechanic in the Air Force from 1961 to 1974, during which time he had assignments in South Korea, Thailand, and Vietnam. (Courtesy of Alabama Department of Archives and History.)

Born in Florence, Alabama, in 1926, Fran McKee gained fame as the first female line officer promoted to rear admiral in the US Navy. The University of Alabama alumna (1950) held multiple assignments and positions before her promotion to flag rank. She earned her first star in 1976 and her second star in 1978. (Courtesy of Alabama Department of Archives and History. Donated by Alabama Media Group. Photograph by Edouard Bruchac, Birmingham News.)

One aspect of the Vietnam War was the capture and retention of downed American pilots. The most famous of the prisoner of war (POW) camps was the "Hanoi Hilton" (Hoa Lo Prison), where pilots, like Navy pilot and future senator John McCain, spent their time in captivity. Negotiations to end the Vietnam War included the return of US pilots. Pictured here is Maj. Glendon W. Perkins speaking at Maxwell Air Force Base in Montgomery upon his return from a prison camp. While the US government states there are no more POWs in Vietnam, there are still over 1,200 military personnel "missing in action" (MIA). (Courtesy of Alabama Department of Archives and History. Donated by Alabama Media Group. Photograph by Robert Adams, Birmingham News.)

Another aspect of the Vietnam War was the large number of refugees. When the United States stopped actively participating in the defense of South Vietnam, North Vietnam forces invaded South Vietnam and united the country after two previous unsuccessful attempts. This action generated a large number of Vietnamese "boat people" who wanted to flee the coming communist regime. The refugees pictured here settled in Mineral Spring, Alabama, in 1975. (Courtesy of Alabama Department of Archives and History. Donated by Alabama Media Group. Photograph by Frank Sikora, Birmingham News.)

The Cold War was not just about directly confronting communism and the Soviet Union; the United States also focused its diplomatic efforts on trying to convince other nations to align with America's democracy. Pictured here are foreign officers from various countries attending military education at Air University at Maxwell Air Force Base, Alabama. (Courtesy of Alabama Department of Archives and History.)

Foreign officers who went through the curriculum at Maxwell Air Force Base were also exposed to other aspects of American culture, including the country's heritage of civilian control of the military. Here, Rotary Club members greet the foreign officers attending Air University. (Courtesy of Alabama Department of Archives and History.)

Alabama did not only supply people to fight the war and provide training areas to train them; it took care of those warfighters as well. Through its mobile canteen, the Salvation Army provided snacks and drinks to those in uniform. (Courtesy of Alabama Department of Archives and History.)

The United Service Organizations (USO) provide relief and aid to those in uniform. Here, servicemembers find rest and necessary services at a USO travelers' aid lounge in Montgomery, Alabama. (Courtesy of Alabama Department of Archives and History.)

Madera Spencer joined the *Montgomery Advertiser* newspaper in 1955 as the society and fashion editor, but her impact would go well beyond the columns she wrote for over 27 years. In 1958, she accompanied an Alabama National Guard unit to its training in Florida and published an article on the unit in the Alabama National Guard magazine. Pres. Richard Nixon appointed Spencer for three years to the Defense Advisory Committee on Women in the Services. The second photograph shows Spencer being briefed on Women in the Air Force facilities at Maxwell Air Force Base by Capt. Shirley Daniel (left) and airman first class Rose Lemar (right). (Courtesy of Alabama Department of Archives and History.)

Five

OTHER COLD WAR FRONTS
FAMILIES, PROTESTS, AND OLYMPICS

The Cold War played out on multiple fronts from 1946 until December 1991, when Pres. George H.W. Bush and Soviet general secretary Mikhail Gorbachev declared the end of the contest. Nuclear weapons arsenals, proxy wars, and the race for space had all been fronts in this ideological conflict. These were the main fronts of the Cold War; however, every facet of life could be made into a competition.

In the global battle to prove the superiority of the US model of government, economics, and culture, family structure became a source of strength for America. Ironically, in the age of atomic weapons, the "nuclear family" became a perceived source of strength. As soldiers returned home from the war, a "baby boom" occurred. The nuclear family needed things to help its growing family, and Alabama manufacturing helped supply that need.

As the Cold War progressed, not everyone in American society supported the US efforts to confront communism everywhere it reared its head. Although the allies emerged victorious in World War II, America would institute drafts to fight the proxy wars in Korea as well as Vietnam. As the baby boomer children grew and attended college, they protested US intervention policies on college campuses around the country, including at colleges in Alabama. Protests against the Vietnam War would expand beyond Alabama universities to the state capitol.

Another front worth noting in the Cold War was athletic competition. While the Olympics always showcase international competition, the quadrennial event took on special meaning during the Cold War. Soviet athletes competed against American athletes with patriotic and political values woven into each event victory. Alabama would have several athletes compete and bring home medals during this period.

After a few decades, the contest seemed like it would endure forever. In 1980, however, America elected California governor Ronald Reagan as the 40th president of the United States. Reagan ran on a platform of prevailing against the "evil empire" (his term for the Soviet Union). Using increased defense spending and diplomatic confrontation, Reagan attempted to bring closure to the Cold War. His efforts put America on a course to victory, but it would be his successor, George H.W. Bush, who would oversee the end of the Cold War.

The return of American troops from World War II led to a baby boom in America, and the "nuclear family"—a father, mother, and multiple children—became a staple of American culture. Television shows like *Leave It to Beaver* and *The Donna Reed* show highlighted the importance of the family in US society. The population growth in America led to the need for labor-saving devices to support family growth like dishwashers, washing machines, dryers, and so on and gave rise to consumerism in America. Alabama contributed to manufacturing items for the growing population. (Courtesy of iStock Photos.)

The Welsh Company of the South had a plant in Union Springs, Alabama, that manufactured strollers, a necessity for the growing family. Above, several workers man the assembly line making strollers and then pack boxes with the finished product for distribution. These pictures highlight the desegregated line operation in Union Springs. (Courtesy of Alabama Department of Archives and History.)

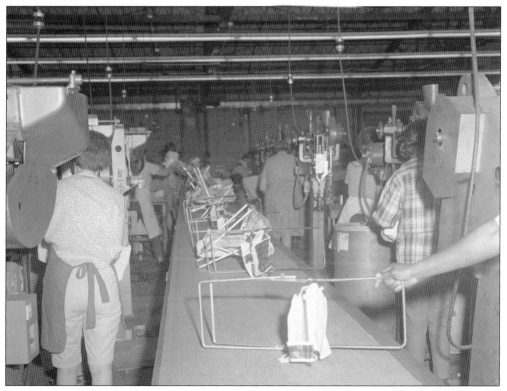

Perhaps no product defines America more than Coca-Cola, and Alabama produced that popular beverage as well. In Montgomery, the Coca-Cola Company had a bottling plant on the corner of North Perry and East Jefferson Streets. In the pictures above, the Montgomery bottling plant holds an open house to commemorate the company's 50th anniversary in the city. A baby boomer child can be seen enjoying a bottle of Coke. (Courtesy of Alabama Department of Archives and History.)

President Eisenhower served as the supreme allied commander in World War II and is largely credited with orchestrating the victory over the Axis foes in Europe. In 1952, "Ike" decided to run for president; this picture is from a campaign stop in Alabama. During his two terms, he made critical decisions on the need for ballistic missiles. He took other actions in the Cold War to highlight the cultural differences between the two superpowers. (Alabama Department of Archives and History. Donated by Alabama Media Group. Photograph by Tom Self, Ed Jones, Bob Gunthorpe, Anthony Falletta, and Eldred Perry, Birmingham News.)

During his first term in office, President Eisenhower took several steps to draw a contrast between the United States and the atheistic Soviet Union over religion. He fought to have "under God" inserted in the Pledge of Allegiance, and on July 30, 1956, he signed into law a bill making "In God We Trust" the national motto, which would be printed on US currency. (Courtesy of iStock Photos.)

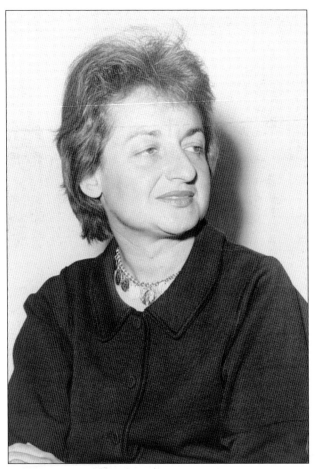

America emphasized the nuclear family and commercialism in the 1950s, but a graduate of Smith College, Betty Friedan lifted the veil on the truth surrounding the role of women in the home. After attending a reunion at her alma mater in 1957 and talking to her female classmates, Friedan would expand her research population and eventually write *The Feminine Mystique*, which exposed how women felt stifled, constrained, and even depressed by their new role in society. Her book and writings would give rise to a second wave of feminism emphasizing reproductive rights, domestic violence, and equality in the workplace. Supporters of feminism at Auburn University are seen hosting an information table in front of the Haley Center. (Above, courtesy of the Library of Congress; below, courtesy of Alabama Department of Archives and History. Donated by Alabama Media Group. Photograph by Charles Nesbitt, Birmingham News.)

The war in Vietnam evoked many protests across the United States. It began in the 1960s and extended well into the 1970s. As the draft continued, many expressed their objection to the war. Above, protestors take to the streets in downtown Birmingham. (Courtesy of Alabama Department of Archives and History. Donated by Alabama Media Group. Photograph by Edouard Bruchac and Charles Nesbitt, Birmingham News.)

Demonstrations against the war and US policies would reach Alabama universities. Students protested administration policies that restricted free speech and political action on campus. In Tuscaloosa, the "People's Movement for a Free Quad" took on the University of Alabama administration's attempts to limit student protests or institute a curfew. (Courtesy of Alabama Department of Archives and History. Donated by Alabama Media Group. Photograph by Frank Sikora, Birmingham News.)

The Tet offensive by the North Vietnamese Army highlighted the failure of US policy and actions in South Vietnam. President Nixon won the election in 1968 with a promise to end the war in Vietnam, but two years later, America was still embroiled in the conflict. On April 15, 1970, several demonstrators met in Woodrow Wilson Park in Birmingham to continue the protest against the war. (Courtesy of Alabama Department of Archives and History. Donated by Alabama Media Group. Photograph by Edouard Bruchac and Charles Nesbitt, Birmingham News.)

On May 4, 1970, Ohio National Guardsmen clashed with antiwar protestors at Kent State University. In the aftermath, four demonstrators were killed, and several were wounded. At the University of Alabama at Birmingham, students display a banner of support for those Kent State protestors and the right of students to protest on campus. (Courtesy of Alabama Department of Archives and History. Donated by Alabama Media Group. Photograph by Ed Jones, Birmingham News.)

Kent State ignited several additional protests across Alabama. On May 11, 1970, another group of protesters would assemble in Birmingham's Woodrow Wilson Park to emphasize first amendment rights. An unidentified little girl at the demonstration carries a sign drawing attention to these the rights of American citizens promised in the First Amendment. . (Courtesy of Alabama Department of Archives and History. Donated by Alabama Media Group. Photograph by Haywood Paravicini, Birmingham News.)

On May 22, 1970, students at Auburn University protested the Vietnam War, showing their solidarity with the Kent State demonstrators. They carried signs that called for an end to US involvement in the conflict. (Courtesy of Alabama Department of Archives and History. Donated by Alabama Media Group. Photograph by Charles Nesbitt, Birmingham News.)

Students at Auburn University, as well as college students across Alabama and the United States, were not unified in the calls for an end to the war. Young Republicans also stood outside Haley Center and had fellow students sign a petition in support of President Nixon and his policies in Vietnam. (Courtesy of Alabama Department of Archives and History. Donated by Alabama Media Group. Photograph by Charles Nesbitt, Birmingham News.)

Support for President Nixon and his policy toward Vietnam would gain support from campus Republicans. There was a noted shift in Alabama politics writ large. Frustrated with the desegregation policies and other actions of Northern Democrats, the South would eventually become a Republican stronghold. (Courtesy of Alabama Department of Archives and History. Donated by Alabama Media Group. Photograph by Charles Nesbitt, Birmingham News.)

Conservatives demonstrated against campus policies and actions. On May 28, 1970, hundreds of students, feeling that the Auburn yearbook featured too many of the campus "hippies," burned the book while roasting marshmallows over the fire. (Courtesy of Alabama Department of Archives and History. Donated by Alabama Media Group. Photograph by Elizabeth Boone Aiken, Birmingham News.)

On May 2, 1971, actress and noted Vietnam War protestor Jane Fonda addressed students at the University of Alabama during a Black History week event. Fonda would later earn the nickname "Hanoi Jane" for her controversial tour of North Vietnam in 1972. While in Hanoi, North Vietnam, she was photographed sitting in an anti-aircraft gun position, which drew heavy criticism in the United States. (Courtesy of Alabama Department of Archives and History. Donated by Alabama Media Group. Photograph by Bob Bass, Birmingham News.)

Conservative University of Alabama students protested the anti-war effort and the "hippie" culture. On May 13, 1970, students, both liberal and conservative, protested outside Alabama's student union. When demonstrators refused to disperse, police arrested 57 protestors. University president David Matthews set a campus-wide curfew and ban on student gatherings. (Courtesy of Alabama Department of Archives and History. Donated by Alabama Media Group. Photograph by Clint Claybrook, Birmingham News.)

The Olympics became a point of contestation between the two global superpowers. At the winter and summer Olympic games, the United States and the Soviet Union put their best athletes forward to compete for Olympic gold as well as political clout. Tuscaloosa native Otis Davis won two gold medals at the 1960 Summer Olympics for the 400 meters and the 4-by-400-meter relay. Following military service in the Air Force during the Korean War, Davis attended the University of Oregon (1958) on a basketball scholarship but ended up trying out track and field. (Courtesy of Italy, unidentified author.)

Born in 1959 in Langdale, Jennifer Chandler was another Alabama athlete who brought home a gold medal from the summer Olympics. At the age of 17, she made it to the Olympic podium for her performance on the three-foot springboard. Here, Chandler is being interviewed at the Talladega 500 race at the Alabama Motor Speedway on her return from capturing Olympic gold. (Courtesy of Alabama Department of Archives and History. Donated by Alabama Media Group. Photograph by Robert Adams, Birmingham News.)

The Olympic career of Ambrose "Rowdy" Gaines highlighted how politics played a role in international competition. Born in Winter Haven, Florida, he attended Auburn University on a swimming scholarship. Although Gaines qualified for the 1980 Summer Olympics, Pres. Jimmy Carter had America boycott the games in protest for the Soviet Union's invasion of Afghanistan. Rowdy would have to qualify again in four years for the summer games being held in Los Angeles, California. In protest of US actions in 1980, the Soviet Union did not attend the 1984 summer games. Gaines would go on to win three gold medals in swimming that summer. (Courtesy of Alabama Department of Archives and History. Donated by Alabama Media Group. Photograph by Haywood Paravicini, Birmingham News.)

Ronald Reagan became largely credited with ending the Cold War. An energy crisis, a hostage crisis in Iran, and unpopular fiscal policies led to his election in 1980. Reagan ran on a platform of prevailing against the Soviet Union by investing in defense and directly confronting the Soviets. In a 1983 speech before the National Association of Evangelicals, Reagan called the Soviet Union "the Evil Empire." Above, a crowd gathers under a banner welcoming candidate Ronald Reagan to Birmingham during his first presidential campaign. In the other picture, President Reagan addresses a joint session of the Alabama legislature attended by (from left to right) senate president pro tempore Finis St. John III, Speaker of the House Joe McCorquodale, Lt. Gov. George McMillan, and Gov. Fob James. (Above, courtesy of Alabama Department of Archives and History. Donated by Alabama Media Group. Photograph by Tom Self, Birmingham News; below, courtesy of Alabama Department of Archives and History. Donated by Alabama Media Group. Photograph by Robert Adams, Birmingham News.)

In June 1987, President Reagan gave a speech outside the Brandenburg Gate of the Berlin Wall asking Soviet secretary general Mikhail Gorbachev to "tear down the wall" that separated democratic West Berlin from communist East Berlin. His desire would become a reality when his successor, George H.W. Bush, took office. On November 9, 1989, the Berlin Wall, which had held many captive to communism, fell. Graffiti now covers the structure that at one time epitomized the Cold War. (Courtesy of iStock Photos.)

Pres. George H.W. Bush oversaw the actual end of the Cold War. In December 1991, after witnessing the fall of the Berlin Wall and the US victory in Operation Desert Storm, Gorbachev and Bush would officially call an end to the Cold War. In April 1991, President Bush attended the weigh-in for the Eagles of Angling Senior Bass Tournament in Pintlala, Alabama. (Courtesy of Alabama Department of Archives and History. Donated by Alabama Media Group. Photograph by Mike Bolton, Birmingham News.)

BIBLIOGRAPHY

Deaile, Melvin G. *Always at War: Organizational Culture in Strategic Air Command, 1946–62*. Annapolis, MD: Naval Institute Press, 2018.

Dudziak, Mary L. *Cold War Civil Rights: Race and the Image of American Democracy*. Princeton, NJ: Princeton University Press, 2000.

Friedan, Betty. *The Feminine Mystique*. Manhattan, NY: W.W. Norton and Company, 1963.

Gaddis, John Lewis. *The Cold War: A New History*. New York, NY: Penguin Press, 2005.

Hamilton, John C. *The Space Race: The Thrilling History of NASA's Race to the Moon*. Eden Prairie, MN: Ravenfire Media, 2019.

McWhorter, Diane. *Carry Me Home: Birmingham, Alabama: The Climatic Battle of the Civil Rights Revolution*. New York, NY: Simon and Schuster, 2001.

Miller, David. *The Cold War: A Military History*. New York, NY: Thomas Dunne, 1999.

Moore, Harold G. and Joseph Galloway. *We Were Soldiers Once . . . and Young: Ia Drang–The Battle That Changed the War in Vietnam*. New York, NY: Random House, 1992.

Neufeld, Michael J. *Von Braun: Dreamer of Space, Engineer of War*. New York, NY: Knopf Publishing, 2007.

Redihan, Erin Elizabeth. *The Olympics and the Cold War, 1948–1968: Sport as Battleground in the US-Soviet Rivalry*. Jefferson, NC: McFarland and Company, 2017.

Discover Thousands of Local History Books Featuring Millions of Vintage Images

Arcadia Publishing, the leading local history publisher in the United States, is committed to making history accessible and meaningful through publishing books that celebrate and preserve the heritage of America's people and places.

Find more books like this at
www.arcadiapublishing.com

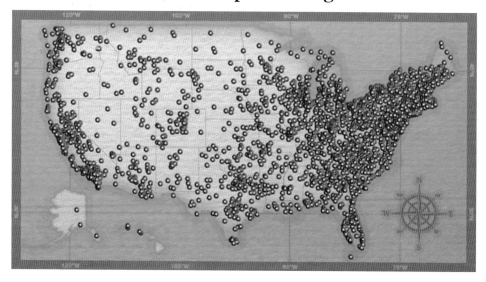

Search for your hometown history, your old stomping grounds, and even your favorite sports team.

Consistent with our mission to preserve history on a local level, this book was printed in South Carolina on American-made paper and manufactured entirely in the United States. Products carrying the accredited Forest Stewardship Council (FSC) label are printed on 100 percent FSC-certified paper.

MADE IN THE USA